ERRAT

JD OCT 94

By the same author

Shibboleth (OUP, 1988)

ERRATA

MICHAEL DONAGHY

Oxford   New York

OXFORD UNIVERSITY PRESS

1993

Oxford University Press, Walton Street, Oxford OX2 6DP

Oxford New York Toronto
Delhi Bombay Calcutta Madras Karachi
Kuala Lumpur Singapore Hong Kong Tokyo
Nairobi Dar es Salaam Cape Town
Melbourne Auckland Madrid
and associated companies in
Berlin Ibadan

Oxford is a trade mark of Oxford University Press

British Library Cataloguing in Publication Data
Data available

Library of Congress Cataloging in Publication Data
Donaghy, Michael.
Errata/Michael Donaghy.
p. cm.—(Oxford poets)
I. Title. II. Series.
PS3554.04635E77 1993 821'.914—dc20 92-25498
ISBN 0-19-283088-0

Typeset by Rowland Phototypesetting Ltd
Printed in Hong Kong

for Maddy Paxman

Acknowledgements

Acknowledgements are gratefully made to the Arts Council of Great Britain, and to the editors of the following anthologies and periodicals in which some of these poems have appeared: *The Sunday Times, Poetry (Chicago), The New Statesman & Society, Poetry Review*, the *Times Literary Supplement, The Honest Ulsterman, Verse, The Jacaranda Review, The Poetry Book Society Anthology 1991–92.*

'Liverpool' was commissioned for BBC radio's *Kaleidoscope* programme.

Several of the poems were first published by the Silver Buckle Press, University of Wisconsin–Madison Libraries, in a limited edition chapbook, *O'Ryan's Belt.*

Contents

I

PLACES IN THE TEMPLE

Held

Not in the sense that this snapshot, a girl in a garden,
Is named for its subject, or saves her from ageing,
Not as this ammonite changed like a sinner to minerals
Heavy and cold on my palm is immortal,
But as we stopped for the sound of the lakefront one morning
Before the dawn chorus of sprinklers and starlings.

Not as this hieroglyph chiselled by Hittites in lazuli,
Spiral and faint, is a word for 'unending',
Nor as the hands, crown, and heart in the emblem of Claddagh,
Pewter and plain on that ring mean forever,
But as we stood at the window together, in silence,
Precisely twelve minutes by candlelight waiting for thunder.

Acts of Contrition

There's you, behind the red curtain,
waiting to absolve me in the dark.
Here's me, third in the queue outside
the same deep green velvet curtain.
I'm working on my confessional tone.

Here's me opening my wrists
before breakfast, Christmas day,
and here's you asking if it hurt.
Here's where I choose between *mea culpa*
and *Why the hell should I tell you?*

Me again, in the incident room this time,
spitting my bloody teeth into your palm.
I could be anyone you want me to be.
I might come round to your point of view.

The Incense Contest

Are you awake, my sweet barbarian?
Why, you look as though you'd seen a ghost!
Are you so shocked to see a lady smoke?
I owe this habit to the Prince, my husband.
That interests you? But that was years ago,
When high-born women told the time by crickets
And generals burned perfumes in their helmets
The night before they rode their troops to battle.
Among the rich it was considered proper
For gentlemen to keep some trace of court
About them in the sweat and shit and smoke.
Among our set those days, in fact, the game
Of 'Guess the Incense' was the latest rage.
Played, like all our games, in grace and earnest,
By intricate directions, for high stakes.

And crispest winter evenings were the best
Because the air is cleanest in the cold.
Without music, badinage, or flowers,
With all attention focused on the flame,
We'd kneel and sniff, and sigh in recognition,
Or we'd pretend, to save a reputation,
Or gamble on assent when someone twigged
'Why this is *Plum Tree Blossom* mixed with balsam.'
On such a night the Empress proposed
An incense contest for the Heian ladies.

We worked for weeks refining subtleties
Of clove and cinnamon and sandalwood,
Selecting lacquers for the bowls and burners
And stiff kimonos for our serving girls.
Imagine generals in midnight camps
Nudging sticks and pebbles across maps;
Just so we worried over strategies
Until the evening of the second snow.

That night we drank the Empress's *sake*.
The Prince, my husband, danced and spoke
A poem written by my grandfather:

> *Shadows on your screens;*
> *a document inked in script*
> *I will yet master.*

A very famous poem. You smile, my lord,
But I come from a literary line.

The alcove, I recall, was full of courtiers
Brushing snow from silken hunting vests
And ladies hushing them. A fan was flicked
To signify the contest had commenced.

First my cousin knelt above the brazier
And blent two scents together on the fire.
Eagles in Winter Light, I think,
And *Village of the Pines* with bergamot.
At first I found her effort elegant,
Warm and old and calm. But moments later,
Barbed and pungent with an old resentment.
The Empress nodded, and glancing toward my husband
Misquoted one of my grandfather's lines.

Next my sister burnt an amber resin
Suggesting pavements after summer rain.
We all felt something which we couldn't name
But which we all agreed was sad and cold
And distant, like some half-remembered grief
From girlhood, or a herb like marjoram.
Once more her Majesty addressed the Prince,
'You seem to have remarkably broad taste.'
And looked at me with something worse than pity.
I knew I'd lost. And when it was my turn
To add my clichéd fragrance to the fire
A door slid open deep within my head . . .

But how can I describe what happened then?
Except to say the blind must dream. They smell
And touch and taste and hear; and you, my dear,
Can dream—are dreaming even now, perhaps—
While all about you swirls a hidden world
Where memories contend like hungry ghosts.
I didn't smell my incense in the brazier:
I smelled the forest and I smelled the horses,
The dung in stables, women giving birth,
The rotting teeth of footmen from the provinces,
The coppery reek of blood, the clogged latrines,
The foetid corpses of the foreign priests
My husband crucified at Gyotoku.
I smelled so many women on the Prince
I smelled the Prince on every woman there.

Are you awake? For if it please you, lord,
To hold that candle just beneath my pipe
Until the black tar glows . . .
                            There. I smoke
To keep those smells at bay. It isn't free,
My dear barbarian, so don't forget
To demonstrate that generosity
For which your noble race is celebrated.
The crickets signal dawn. Time to rise
And face the sun and leave me to my dream.

Glass

This is a cheapjack gift at the year's end.
This is a double-glazing hymn for wind.
This is a palm frond held out to a friend
Who holds her lifeline lightly in her hand.

As fine sand filaments the unclenched hand
Or leaves the palm grit-filmed but crazed, lines end
Across prismatic windscreens. Every friend
A meteorologist's diagram of wind.

Blow smoke into the fist of either hand
And pull it tight and loop it round the end
Of every night held up by wine and friend,
Sootflecked and leaning on a London wind,

Then say our ribboned smoke's erased by wind,
Our glass is sand. You start, but in the end,
Somehow, I stay. You stay, somehow, my friend
Who grips me tightest in her open hand.

The Commission

In spring when the mountain snows melt
and the western wind crumbles
and loosens the clods, in the spring
when the bees roam incontinently
over the glades and the woodlands,
I returned to the plague-levelled city
to cut off the head of the man
who had murdered my brother.

To cover my purpose and pay off my debts
I set up a shop in the Via Rigoglio
and accepted a papal commission.
In the evenings I shadowed
the arquebusier Ludovico
like a love-smitten boy,
watching his house,
his comings and goings.

Pope Clement had ordered three follies:
a spindly gold locust that chirruped and kicked
on release of a mainspring,
an amethyst brooch,
and a nine-inch stiletto
with monogrammed handle in findrinny
and he wanted a cameo laid in its pommel:
Hercules binding the three-headed Cerberus.

To help me I hired a silversmith
known as Filippo, whose idiot daughter
I kept in the shop to amuse me. But
during that summer she fell in a fever.
Her hand was diseased. Both the bones of her thumb
and ring finger were eaten away.
I'd received an advance from the Pope
so I sent for the finest of surgeons.

She screamed when he started
to scrape away some of the bone
using a crude iron tool, and since
I could see he was making no progress
I got him to stop for five minutes. I ran
to the workshop and fashioned
a delicate instrument, steel, curved,
tiny and sharp as a razor.

This I gave to the surgeon
who now worked so gently
the girl felt no pain.
Filippo in gratitude made me a gift
of a dagger he'd chanced on in Persia.
He knew I would find the design on the handle
compelling—the name of their god
swirling like silvery foliage.

(The ignorant call such engravings 'grotesques'
because they resemble the carvings in grottoes.
This is an error. For just as the ancients
created their monsters
by mating with bulls and with horses,
so we artists create our own monsters
in networks of intertwined branches and leaves.)

I finally found Ludovico alone
on the night of the feast of St Mark.
It was pissing down rain and the bells
of S. Paolo were striking eleven.
I crept up behind as he stood
in a doorway in Torre Sanguigna
and brought down the silversmith's dagger
as hard as I could on his nape

but he turned and I shattered his shoulder.
Blinded with pain he let go of his sword
and again I went straight for his neck,
and this time the blade stuck so deep that it snapped
at the hilt. Then he fell to his knees
and stared at me stupidly, clutching the knife
as if he were trying to keep me away from it.
I looked in his eyes until I was sure they were empty.
Then footsteps. I broke off the handle and ran.

I was suspected of course, so I kept out of sight
and worked day and night for the Pope
as I had no desire to spend August in Rome
or get myself hanged.
When I finally brought him his toys
he was propped up in bed
being bled. But he granted an audience.
Jaundice. His flesh was like cheese.

When I laid out my labours before him
he squinted and sent for his spectacles,
then for more lamps. But it was no use.
He was blind as a mole.
Most of the time he spent sighing
and praising my godgiven talent,
thumbing that wretched mechanical insect.

He almost ignored the stiletto
on which, from the figure of Hercules down,
I'd copied the Persian device from the dagger
that brought me such luck, disguising
the writing as branches.

By Christmas Pope Clement was dead.
And all of my efforts to stay in his favour
were wasted, which just goes to show
how completely the stars rule our lives.

Cruising Byzantium

The saved, say firemen, sometimes return,
Enduring the inferno of the flat
To fetch the family photos. And they burn
Not for cash, cashmere coat, nor cat,
Nor, as they momently suppose, for love.
They perish for the heraldries of light
And not such lives as these are emblem of.
But the saved, say firemen, are sometimes right.

Have you seen our holiday snaps from Greece?
Each Virgin burns in incandescent wonder
From her gold mosaic altarpiece.
This one was smashed by Gothic boot boys under
Orders from an Emperor who burned
The icon painters for idolatry.
Before her ruined face the faithful learned
The comet's path to a celestial sea.
And look. Here's *you* in skintight scuba gear
Winking through the window of your mask!
You have become the fetish that you wear.
I know precisely what you're going to ask;
Though golden in the Adriatic haze
You've waded to your thighs in molten light,
Your second skin aglitter in the sprays,
Your first it was we brought to bed that night.
And yet I'd almost brave the flames to keep
This idyll of perversity from burning.

Each photo frames a door beyond which, deep
Within the Patriarchate of my yearning,
The marble pavements surge with evensong.
But firemen say the saved are sometimes wrong.

City of God

When he failed the seminary he came back home
to the Bronx and sat in a back pew
of St Mary's every night reciting the Mass
from memory—quietly, continually—
into his deranged overcoat.
He knew the local phone book off by heart.
He had a system, he'd explain,
perfected by Dominicans in the Renaissance.

To every notion they assigned a saint,
to every saint an altar in a transept of the church.
Glancing up, column by column, altar by altar,
they could remember any prayer they chose.
He'd used it for exams, but the room went wrong—
a strip-lit box exploding slowly as he fainted.
They found his closet papered floor to ceiling
with razored passages from St Augustine.

He needed a perfect cathedral in his head,
he'd whisper, so that by careful scrutiny
the mind inside the cathedral inside the mind
could find the secret order of the world
and remember every drop on every face
in every summer thunderstorm.
And that, he'd insist, looking beyond you,
is why he came home.

I walked him back one evening as the snow
hushed the precincts of his vast invisible temple.
Here was Bruno Street where Bernadette
collapsed, bleeding through her skirt
and died, he had heard, in a state of mortal sin;

here, the site of the bakery fire where Peter stood
screaming on the red hot fire escape,
his bare feet blistering before he jumped;
and here the storefront voodoo church beneath the el
where the Cuban *bruja* bought black candles,
its window strange with plaster saints and seashells.

Liverpool

Ever been tattooed? It takes a whim of iron,
takes sweating in the antiseptic-stinking parlour,
nothing to read but motorcycle magazines
before the blood-sopped cotton and, of course, the needle,
all for—at best—some Chinese dragon.
But mostly they do hearts,

hearts skewered, blurry, spurting like the Sacred Heart
on the arms of bikers and sailors.
Even in prison they get by with biro ink and broken glass,
carving hearts into their arms and shoulders.
But women's are more intimate. They hide theirs,
under shirts and jeans, in order to bestow them.

Like Tracy, who confessed she'd had hers done
one legless weekend with her ex.
Heart. Arrow. Even the bastard's initials, R.J.L.,
somewhere where it hurt, she said,
and when I asked her where, snapped 'Liverpool'.

Wherever it was, she'd had it sliced away
leaving a scar, she said, pink and glassy,
but small, and better than having his mark on her,

(that self-same mark of Valentinus,
who was flayed for love, but who never
—so the cardinals now say—existed.
Desanctified, apocryphal, like Christopher,
like the scar you never showed me, Trace,
your (   ), your ex, your 'Liverpool').

Still, when I unwrap the odd anonymous note
I let myself believe that it's from you.

L

'Switch off the engine and secure the car.'
He slots his pen across his clipboard
and makes a little cathedral of his fingers
as though I were helping him with his enquiries.
'Tell me, Michael, what's your line of work?'

I tell him the truth. Why not? I've failed anyway.
'Driving and writing have a lot in common,'
he parleys, and we sit there, the two of us
blinking into the average braking distance
for 30 mph, wondering what he means.

I want to help but it's his turn to talk.
When my turn comes he'll probably look at me
instead of his hand, stalled now in mid-gesture
like a milkfloat halfway across a junction.
Look at him. What if I'd said *butcher*?

At last 'It's all a matter of giving—proper—signals'
is the best he can do. But then he astonishes me.
'I'm going to approve your licence,
but I don't care much for your . . .' Quick glance.
'*interpretation* of the Highway Code.'

Alas, Alice,

who woke to crows and woke up on the ceiling and hung there fearing
the evening's sweeping and looked down now at her unfinished reading
and loved by sleeping and slept by weeping and called out once. The
words were dust. Who left late singing and signed up leaving and ran
home slowly afraid of sleeping and hated thinking and thought by feeling
and called out once but no one came,

who dreamt blue snow and froze in dreaming and spoke by reading and
read all evening and read by patterns of blizzards drifting and dared by
waiting and waited taking and called out once and called out twice and
coughed grey clouds and carved four coffins and took by thanking and
thanked by seeking and drifted bedwards and lay there weeping and
counted her tears and divided by seven and called out once. The words
were crows.

A Discourse on Optics

i   the heirloom

Now its silver paint is flaking off,
That full-length antique bevelled mirror
Wants to be clear water in a trough,
Still, astringent water in November.

It worked for sixty years, day and night
Becoming this room and its passing faces.
Holding it now against the light
I see the sun shines through in places.

It wants to be the window that it was,
Invisible as pleasure or pain,
Framing whatever the day may cause—
The moon. A face. Rain.

I'll prop it up outside against the skip
So clouds can ghost across the rust.
Though I can't see myself in it,
Still, it's·the only mirror that I trust.

ii   the pond

The shape of man, a shadow on the ground,
Returns, a mirror image, from pondwater.
So it is we think the soul not shade,
Not silhouette, but solid matter.

Except those times light strikes the basin level
And almost makes a window of the surface
To show our shadow amid coins and gravel
Outgazing the sad overcoat and face,

To teach them, I suppose, they are that darkness
Deepening the bottom of the pool,
And teach the soul it wears the face and coat
Which that lucidity obscures.

26

II

O'RYAN'S BELT

The Hunter's Purse

is the last unshattered 78
by 'Patrolman Jack O'Ryan, violin',
a Sligo fiddler in dry America.

A legend, he played Manhattan's ceilidhs,
fell asleep drunk one snowy Christmas
on a Central Park bench and froze solid.
They shipped his corpse home, like his records.

This record's record is its lunar surface.
I wouldn't risk my stylus to this gouge,
or this crater left by a flick of ash—

When Anne Quinn got hold of it back in Kilrush,
she took her fiddle to her shoulder
and cranked the new Horn of Plenty
Victrola over and over and over,
and scratched along until she had it right
or until her father shouted

> 'We'll have *no* more
> Of *that* tune
> In *this* house to*night*.'

She slipped out back and strapped the contraption
to the parcel rack and rode her bike
to a far field, by moonlight.

It skips. The penny I used for ballast slips.
O'Ryan's fiddle pops, and hiccoughs
back to this, back to this, back to this:
a napping snowman with a fiddlecase;
a flask of bootleg under his belt;
three stars; a gramophone on a pushbike;
a cigarette's glow from a far field;
over and over, three bars in common time.

A Repertoire

'Play us one we've never heard before'
we'd ask this old guy in our neighborhood.
He'd rosin up a good three or four
seconds, stalling, but he always could.
This was the Bronx in 1971,
when every night the sky was pink with arson.
He ran a bar beneath the el, the Blarney Stone,
and there one Easter day he sat us down
and made us tape as much as he could play;
'I gave you these. Make sure you put that down',
meaning all he didn't have to say.

All that summer we slept on fire escapes,
or tried to sleep, while sirens or the brass
from our neighbour's Tito Puente tapes
kept us up and made us late for mass.
I found our back door bent back to admit
beneath the thick sweet reek of grass
a nest of needles, bottlecaps, and shit.
By August Tom had sold the Blarney Stone
to Puerto Ricans, paid his debts in cash
but left enough to fly his body home.

The bar still rises from the South Bronx ash,
its yellow neon buzzing in the noonday
dark beneath the el, a sheet-steel door
bolted where he played each second Sunday.
'Play me one I've never heard before'
I'd say, and whether he recalled those notes
or made them up, or—since it was Tom who played—
whether it was something in his blood
(cancer, and he was childless and afraid)
I couldn't tell you. And he always would.

A Reprieve

'Realizing that few of the many tunes remembered from boyhood days . . . were known to the galaxy of Irish musicians domiciled in Chicago, the writer decided to have them preserved in musical notation. This was the initial step in a congenial work which has filled in the interludes of a busy and eventful life.'

—Police Chief Francis O'Neil, *Irish Folk Music: A Fascinating Hobby, With some Account of Related Subjects* (Chicago 1910)

Here in Chicago it's almost dawn
and quiet in the cell in Deering Street stationhouse
apart from the first birds at the window and the milkwagon
and the soft slap of the club in Chief O'Neil's palm.
'Think it over,' he says, 'but don't take all day.'
Nolan's hands are brown with a Chinaman's blood.
But if he agrees to play three jigs
slowly, so O'Neil can take them down,
he can walk home, change clothes,
and disappear past the stockyards and across the tracks.

Indiana is waiting. O'Neil lowers his eyes,
knowing the Chinaman's face will heal, the Great Lakes
roll in their cold grey sheets and wake,
picket lines will be charged, girls raped
in the sweatshops, the clapboard tenements burn.
And he knows that Nolan will be gone by then,
the coppery stains wiped from the keys of the blackwood flute.

Five thousand miles away Connaught sleeps.
The coast lights dwindle out along the west.
But there's music here in this lamplit cell,
and O'Neil scratching in his manuscript like a monk
at his illuminations, and Nolan's sweet tone breaking
as he tries to phrase a jig the same way twice:
'The Limerick Rake' or 'Tell her I am' or 'My Darling Asleep'.

Theodora, Theodora

Tomorrow, Parnassus. Tonight, outside the taverna,
you wait in the darkened coach alone
flaking *kif* into a roll-up by the dashboard light.
Plates crash. The band risk a verse or two
of a song they played before the war in brothels
where you fucked, gambled, and somehow failed
to die; a song about a girl who didn't.
For love. Slum music. Knives and despair.
Softly you sing what words you can remember.

There are stars in the chorus, and two brothers,
hashish, wisteria, a straight razor. You can't recall
the name of the song or the name of the girl
who bleeds to death at dawn by birdsong before the basilica,
but they're the same. It's been so long.
The bishops banned it, and the colonels,
and somehow even you—how else could you forget—
because these songs have backstreets much like this.
Bile and retsina. Streets the cops don't like.

Sixteen bars then into *Zorba*. The tour-group clap,
snap pictures, then stumble on board laughing
in accents of Buenos Aires or Chicago,
where coach drivers wait outside bars on the south side,
singing softly, for no one but themselves tonight,
of girls who bleed for love. 'Theodora.'
You remember. 'Theodora.' Singing too loud,
you take the slow road back to the hotel.

Down

The stars are shuffling slowly round
Burning in the dark
Upon the lips of angry men
Drinking in the park.
Five thousand fed. I read it in
The Gospel of St Mark.

Helicopters insect round
Above the burned out cars.
Here where Gospel testified
Between the wars
His harp of darkness cried and prayed
To bottleneck guitars.

Tell me why's you cryin' baby?
I sure would like to know.
Tell me why's you cryin' baby?
I sure would like to know.
Some words I can't make out, and then,
I'll come walkin' through that door.

These flattened thirds and sevenths
Justified the Blues:
Intervals ruled by celestial laws,
Horse, and booze.
Woke up this morning's just the kind
Of line he couldn't use.

Cicadas carve across this night
Their lapidary phrase,
And the darkness children fear
They continually praise.
The darkness children fear, they
Continually praise.

The Classics

I remember it like it was last night,
Chicago, the back room of Flanagan's
malignant with accordions and cigarettes,
Joe Cooley bent above his Paolo Soprani,
its asthmatic bellows pumping as if to revive
the half-corpse strapped about it.
It's five a.m. Everyone's packed up.
His brother Seamus grabs Joe's elbow mid-arpeggio.
'Wake up man. We have to catch a train.'
His eyelids fluttering, opening. The astonishment . . .

I saw this happen. Or heard it told so well
I've staged the whole drunk memory:
What does it matter now? It's ancient history.
Who can name them? Where lie their bones and armour?

III

TRUE

The Chamber of Errors

It never gets as crowded as Tussaud's,
But every day we draw the curious few
Who've seen our sticker on the underground,
Our card in a phone box, and felt
That, somehow, it was printed just for them.
Of course, it was. Step in and look around.
You haven't come for Marilyn or Elvis.
Like you, I loathe that taxidermal bathos.
We use the faces left in photobooths
By rushed commuters. Their eyes already closed,
We only have to make them *look* like wax.

Now look you on the unfamiliar dead.
More than the pancaked meat in satin caskets,
More than the unforgiving memories,
These are your unforgiven. But be warned,
Like faces glimpsed in fever on the curtains,
These will never truly go away.
Look round, and after, should you need to rest,
And many do, there is a chesterfield.
But please, please, this is important,

Don't touch. I spend my life repairing details.
See where I've pressed the hairs in one by one?
And here? See where I've whorled the fingerpads?
I can't think what possesses people. *Christ*,
Sometimes, at night, I find the faces gouged.

Reliquary

The robot camera enters the Titanic
And we see her fish-cold nurseries on the news;
The toys of Pompeii trampled in the panic;
The death camp barrel of babyshoes;

The snow that covered up the lost girl's tracks;
The scapular she wore about her neck;
The broken doll the photojournalist packs
to toss into the foreground of the wreck.

Ovation

O pilgrim from above led through these flames,
There was a time I looked down on a thousand torches.

My voice brought such an echo of applause
You'd think each word a stone dropped in a well.

Our Land. Splash. *Justice long denied.*
Splash. *The humble exalted*

The exalted . . . and so forth. Immortal words.
It was like love. And my queen loved me,
Could quote my book verbatim.

Then that winter underground, and the golden dream
Defiled by weaklings whispering like burning fat.
Even she was heard to whisper, my Isolde.

I hanged the astrologer, and slipped beneath my tongue
The key to the drawer in which lay locked
The cyanide, the luger, and my speeches . . .

She would ridicule me in the end,
Quoting them to me verbatim.

Co-Pilot

He leadeth me in the paths of righteousness,
Sitting on my shoulder like a pirate's parrot,
Whispering the decalogue like a tiny Charlton Heston.
Tch, he goes. *Tch Tch*. He boreth me spitless.

Tonight I need a party with a bottomless punchbowl
Brimming cool vodka to the lip of the horizon.
I'll yank him from his perch and hold him under
Until the bubbles stop.

Cage,

The composer, locked in a soundproof room in Harvard
Heard his heartbeat and the sound of Niagara Falls
Produced by the operation of his nervous system,
From which he derived a theory, no doubt.

Me, I heard a throaty click at the end of 'wedlock'.
And Niagara on the long-distance line.
I knew a couple once, went up there on their honeymoon.
After a week, they said, you don't even hear it.

Meridian

There are two kinds of people in the world.
Roughly. First there are the kind who say
'There are two kinds of people in the world'
And then there's those who don't.

Me, I live smack on the borderline,
Where the road ends with towers and searchlights,
And we're kept awake all night by the creak of the barrier
Rising and falling like Occam's razor.

Lives of the Artists

I The Age of Criticism

The clergy, who are prone to vertigo,
Dictate to heaven with a megaphone.
And those addressing Michelangelo
As he was freeing David from the stone
As much as said they thought the nose too big.
He waited till he got them on their own,
Scooped some marble dust up with his tools,
And climbing loftily atop his rig,
He tapped his chisel for those squinting fools
And let a little dust fall on their faces.

He tapped and tapped. And nothing slowly changed
Except for the opinions of Their Graces.

II The Discovery and Loss of Perspective

Her personal vanishing point,
she said, came when she leant
against his study door
all warm and wet and whispered
'Paolo. Bed.'

He only muttered,
gazing down his grid, 'Oh,
what a lovely thing perspective is!'
She went to live
with cousins in Madrid.

III   The Advance of Naturalism

As any dripping clepsydra, batsqueak
In the eaves, or square of angry birds,
So Donatello's steady chisel rhythm
Could sound like words. Perhaps you've read
How someone put his ear against a crack
And heard him try to make a statue speak.
Well, I was there. I heard it answer back.

Of all the cheek! it said, *Show some respect!*
The hand that makes us perfect makes us each
Submissive to the other's intellect.
Nor have we any confidence to teach
Through speaking sculpture or through sculptured speech.

Signifyin' Monkey

'Never write a check with your mouth your ass can't cash.'
—Zach Newton

O.K. I'll tell it, but only if you buy lunch.
One summer I worked nights for Vigil-Guard,
the Chicago security firm. The work was easy:
sitting. And close to home. Ten minutes on the train.
And every night I passed the same fluorescent sign
somewhere in Chinatown: FIGHTER MONKEY.

I paid it no mind. It was the year of the monkey.
I thought I'd try it out one day for lunch.
Risky, I figured, but it's always a good sign
if the sign's in English. I wasn't made chief guard
for nothing, you know. It takes a week to train
on half pay so don't think it's all that easy.
Security's an art. I just make it *look* easy,
like the day I walked home past Fighter Monkey.
Looking back, I wish I'd caught that train,
but I was after a cheap pork feng shui lunch.
Something out front put me on my guard,
though, something about that Day Glo sign,
the smell, and the cages in the windows, and no sign
of a menu anywhere, which made me a little uneasy,
when out steps this white guy built like a bodyguard
wearing a T-shirt showing a shrieking monkey.
He just stands there, chin out. 'Still serving lunch?'
I ask. 'This is no restaurant,' he says. 'I train
animals'—He's got this tight whisper—'I train
Barbary Apes using American Sign
Language.' O.K. I figure he's out to lunch,
a potential situation. 'Take it easy,'
I tell him. 'I made a mistake. *You* train monkeys . . .
I represent a firm called Vigil-Guard.'
Turns out he once trained dogs for Vigil-Guard.
And he pays me there and then to help him train

one of his babies, a kind of Rottweiler monkey
that took her orders and talked back in Sign.
I swear she must have weighed forty pounds easy.
And teeth! She could have had me for lunch.
Shit, she could have had me *and* lunch!
Then he hauls out this heavy, padded armguard.
'Put that on,' he says. 'This part is safe and easy.
She's going to come at you like a freight train.
Freeze.' I remember he laughed as he made the sign.
The asshole. Lost a thumb to his own monkey.

It's easy. Look, he'd been her only trainer.
Guard or no guard, he'd signed 'I'm lunch.'
The blood! Of course they had to shoot the monkey.

Shooting The Crane People

It was a hard year and it was always raining.
The first six months they ran at our approach.
But finally, by patience and cunning,
we gained their trust. Or they learned to ignore us.

Their dialect is noisy and almost unlearnable.
There are no vowels. Their name for themselves,
for example, is a hiss followed by a tiny choking sound
and means 'we', but homophones abound.

Their name for us, a sharp intake of breath,
is also the word for mudslides, or a large, inedible carcass.
We found pronunciation difficult and the slightest error
was met with confusion, irritation, and contempt.

Though excellent telegenic material,
they couldn't recognize themselves on screen.
They move like cranes, and when they squat to dig for grubs
it's like the start of a sad slow dance.

They found our camera terrifying
and were eager to learn to use it.
Our guide would video his wives to punish them.
It was a hard year. I didn't like them. It was always raining.

Banzai

'Our cooking depends upon shadows and is inseparable from darkness.'
—Jun'ichiro Tanizaki

'Don't be nervous. Be hungry.'
Donovan refilled my *sake*.

The chairman was taller than I expected.
He sat at the head of the table,
Donovan between us to translate.

Looking at Donovan, he spoke to me
of risks, profits and futures, and
when Donovan crossed his fingers and winked,
I made my move, surprising myself.
'Tell him I want a taste of power.'
Donovan frowned with the effort.

A chrysanthemum pattern of glassy flesh
arrived which the chairman had ordered for us,
with gravity, several lifetimes earlier—
an expensive, mildly neurotoxic sashimi,
prepared by licensed chefs. Occasionally fatal.
He pincered a morsel, blinked, and swallowed.
Slainte he said, speaking to Donovan, looking at me.

Becoming Catastrophic

Purification itself takes several days. It is agonizing: explosive diarrhoea, sweats, retching, shaking, itching, freezing. But by the second morning the flesh turns white and gradually transparent. Fat, hair, and muscle are the last to go, until finally the tough black dots of the pupils wink out and you see through the world's eyes at last. This is why, having never been corporeal, Thrones, Principalities, Dominions and Powers cannot be depicted except as fortuitous events. Mate in five moves, say. And this is why, once invisible, pains must be taken to think invisibly, for to look too greenly on some sunlit apple's green ebullience can spark a plebiscite, freak hail, sunshower. Remember you are not omnipresent, only infinitely responsible. Always eat alone; your unassimilated food and waste may be visible for hours.

True

n 7 (as of a compass bearing) according to the earth's geographical rather than magnetic poles. True north.
vb 15 (tr) to adjust so as to make true.

i   a grand magic lantern entertainment

ONE NIGHT ONLY

illustrated by over FORTY DISSOLVENT VIEWS of a strictly moral character. Nothing to offend the most fastidious person.

Scriptural Views   Comic Songs and Speeches
Lord Franklin setting out to discover a northwest passage
AROUND THE POLE!

The Esquimeaux of the Labradors are aboriginals with no religious rite. Instead they catch beneath the ice a small, somewhat poisonous silver fish which they consume uncooked. This practice induces fever and vivid dreams, and they prognosticate by reading in the putrified viscera of seals.

Lord Franklin has just read 'Ulysses',
Tennyson's latest, and collapses
his brass collapsible telescope.

> *Twas homeward bound one night on the deep*
> *Swinging in my hammock I fell asleep.*
> *I dreamt a dream and I thought it true*
> *Concerning Franklin and his gallant crew.*

In June, becalmed in sight of a Swedish whaler,
Lord Franklin signalled her captain
to dinner followed by a game of backgammon.
But the long day waned and the sails filled,
and the English waved from the deck
till they were out of sight.
Old age hath yet its honour and its toil.

'One of our visitors held a pocketwatch to his ear. Supposing it to be alive, he asked if it was good to eat. Another, handed a wineglass appeared very much astonished that it did not melt in the heat of his hand as he entertained a notion that it was made of ice.'

ii Franklin missing

With a hundred seamen he sailed away
On the frozen ocean in the month of May.
In Baffin Bay where the whale fish blow
The fate of Franklin no man may know.

'With interest which accumulates by the hour do we watch for the return
of these two vessels which are perhaps even now working their way
through the Bering strait into the Pacific.'

The Sikh boy dims
a fringed gas lamp.
Mme Murphy, the sensitive,
bids Lady Franklin sit.

'Please join hands and empty your minds
of all worldly thoughts.'
She summons the spirit
of Sir John Franklin.

Silence in the perfumed dark.
The carriage clock needs winding.

Swedenborg, she explains,
holds that angels,
being purely selfless beings,
generate rather than take up space.
Jammed wing to wing, the halls of heaven
are vast and empty as the ice pack.

Someone coughs and fidgets.
'Wait . . . I see . . . I see . . .
No more today. Please. The palpitations.
Fetch the ladies' coats Mahapatra,
and show Lord Merryll in.'

iii   the search party

And now my burden it gives me pain
To think my Franklin lies across the Main.
Ten thousand pounds would I freely give
To say on earth that my Franklin does live.

'We pressed on and discovered at four o clock
two skeletons in furs face down in the ice.
We scattered black matchstick bones
from one braided sleeve and found they'd clutched
a toothbrush and a silver medal for navigation
awarded by the Royal Naval College, 1830,
and the remains of a letter of which was legible:

". . . all spoilt. Seven hundret tins in all. Several strong men fainted and
wee drew lots to put out with . . . . . . the long boat to look for free
wather. On the 12th night of our hawl, brother Dick, wee saw 2 very
large hice Burgh to windward of ous and we stopt in thare shadow for to
rest in the boat for the wether was bad and weed be out of the wind.
Apon taking off his boots wee see Capten Hughs has no payne in his feet
and says they feel warm but wee feer he will soon loose them. We are
most blynded from the hice and I feer, dear friends, I canot rite very
longer for my eyes hurt full sore and I am week for want of food. Tell
mother I die a Chrischun in Gods mercee

                    Good by untell we meet in heven,
                              Tom Cook"

For what we found next I regret I can offer
neither explanation nor conjecture,
for we discovered scattered about beneath half-buried sledges
seventy silk handkerchiefs, five pocket watches,
a badminton racket, a birdcage, a tiny clockwork cricket,
a brass telescope, and several barrel organs,
their gearwork still in fair condition.
One of these last I tested, and winding its handle
I succeeded in producing a medley from popular operettas
until a storm blew up and we struck back for camp.'

Privacy

Here, as in life, they were admitted
to a club exclusive as the Garrick,
now a kind of Victorian Angkor Wat
adjacent to the A road.
Their mossed, sepulchral pieties
neglected for decades, swallowed
back into a mild jungle,
their shapeless sculpture decked
flat, sprayed with uncouth rhymes,
their eminent corpses
violated by ritual necrophilia in the 60's,
how fares it with the happy dead?

The PM urges their revival,
the spirits of industry, exploration,
eels and gin, the floorless jig.
Here, everyone knows his place.
Here, little green bronze bells
festoon the exterior of the 'Egyptian' mausoleum.
The strings once led inside,
where, waking in their two inch dark,
the prematurely interred
could tintinnabulate as if for tea.
Sadly, these have snapped.

The Raindial

The sun goes in. The light goes out.
A million shadows fade away.
It could be any time of day.
Now dream that you don't dream about
The garden of this Hackney squat
Where dark drops stipple on the *Sun*,
The umbrella skeleton,
The sink, the broken flowerpot . . .

A cold rain slicks the garden path
That leads you down the overgrowth
Toward the monument to Thoth:
A drowned shark in a birdbath.

Above its fin the zodiac
Spins upon its sentinel.
The gnomon knows, but will not tell
The time nor give your future back.
The gnomon knows. And round it's writ
As these long   pass swift away
So too the hope of man decays.
TippExed under pigeonshit,
The years, the months, the weeks, the days.

The Brother

Dropping a canape in my beaujolais
At some reception, opening or launch,
I recall briefly the brother I never had
Presiding at less worldly rituals:
The only man at my wedding not wearing a tie;
Avuncular, swaddling my nephew over the font;
Thumbing cool oil on our mother's forehead
In the darkened room, the bells and frankincense . . .
While the prodigal sweats in the strip lit corridor.

Now, picture us facing each other, myself and the brother
I never met: two profiles in silhouette,
Or else a chalice, depending how you look.
Imagine that's this polystyrene cup.
I must break bread with my own flesh and blood.

Fraction

The fourteenth time my mother told the story
Of her cousins dismembered by a British bomb,
I turned on her, her Irish son. 'I'm American.
I was born here.' She went to pieces.

And would not be solaced. I had her eyes,
The aunt's, that is, who, the story goes,
Was brought to the jail to sort the bits in tubs.
Toes. I meant to renounce such grotesque pity.

I was thirteen. I didn't know who I was. She knew.
As I held her wrists, reassuring,
Repeating, that I was her Irish son,
I was the man who'd clicked the toggle switch

Bracing himself between two branches,
Between the flash and the report.

Erratum

I touch the cold flesh of a god in the V and A,
the guard asleep in his chair, and I'm shocked
to find it's plaster. These are the reproduction rooms,
where the David stands side by side with the Moses
and Trajan's column (in two halves).
It reminds me of the inventory sequence in *Citizen Kane*.
It reminds me of an evening twenty years ago.

And all at once I'm there, at her side,
turning the pages as she plays
from the yellowed song sheets I rescued from a bookstall:
Dodd's setting of *Antony and Cleopatra*. All very improving.
'Give me my robe and crown,' she warbles
in a Victorian coloratura. 'I have immoral longings in me.'

I want to correct her—the word on the page is
immortal—but I'm fourteen and scandalized.
(I knew there were no innocent mistakes.
I'd finished *Modern Masters: Freud*
before she snatched and burned it. 'Filth'—
yanking each signature free of the spine,
'Filth. Filth. Filth.')

The song is over. But when she smiles at me,
I'm on the verge of tears, staring down at the gap-
toothed grimace of our old Bechstein. 'What's wrong?'
What's *wrong*? I check the word again. She's right. Immoral.
She shows me the printer's slip, infecting
the back page of every copy, like,
she might have said, the first sin.

The guard snorts in his dream. I take my palm away
still cool from what I'd taken to be marble.
And when I get that moment back, it's later;
I'm sobbing on her shoulder and I can't say why.
So she suggests another visit to the furnace, where,
to comfort me, perhaps, we rake the cinders with the music
till they chink and spark, and shove the pages
straight to the white core to watch them darken as if ageing,
blacken, enfold, like a sped-up film of blossoms in reverse.

Some Notes

'The Hunter's Purse'

'Well, they used to come by emigrants coming home on holidays, mostly, because they'd imagine if they posted them they'd be broken, which they would at the time. And it was all returned Americans coming home to see their own native place again that brought both the gramophones and the records. And there was as much lookout for an emigrant returning home that time as there would be for—I don't know what now, to see an aeroplane going into orbit or something off the ground. Because there was an awful lookout for John McKenna's records, an awful lookout.'—Tommy Gilmartin, quoted by Harry Bradshaw and Jackie Small in 'John McKenna, Leitrim's master of the Concert flute' (*Musical Traditions*, No. 7, 1987).

'A Repertoire'

'Play me one we've never heard before.' Chicago fiddler Liz Carroll would ask this of the late Johnny McGreevy who would always comply. But the poem is not about Johnny.

'Theodora, Theodora'

In 'The Gangster Reformed, A study in musical parallels' Jaoa Dos Santos compares the subcultures of Tango, Fado, and Rembetika (*Musical Traditions*, No. 7, 1987). He might also consider the lifespan of urban Blues.

'Down'

What I heard of the song was sung by Jimmy Reed.

'Lives of the Artists'

Three misremembered episodes from Vasari's lives of, respectively, Michelangelo, Uccello, and Donatello. He remarks that the latter used to mutter to his favourite piece, the *Zuccone*, 'Speak, or the plague take you!'

'Signifyin' Monkey'

is the title of an R&B standard. Vigil-Guard were a private security firm on Chicago's west side. Zach Newton was my supervisor there.

'Banzai'

Fugu (*C. riulatus Fugu rubripes* or Pacific pufferfish), if improperly filleted of its liver and roe, causes paralysis and death within minutes.

'True'

Most of it is. The song is a Victorian broadside I got from the singing of Micheal O'Domhnaill. Some of the other quotations are from Ross, Captain John, *A Voyage of Discovery in HM Ships 'Isabella and Alexander'* (John Murray, 1819) and Lord Egerton in the *London Quarterly Review* (June 1847), which is quoted in Evan S. Connell's account of the Franklin expedition in *A Long Desire* (Holt Reinhart and Winston, 1977). Other quotations are trued.

OXFORD POETS

Fleur Adcock
Kamau Brathwaite
Joseph Brodsky
Basil Bunting
Daniela Crăsnaru
W. H. Davies
Michael Donaghy
Keith Douglas
D. J. Enright
Roy Fisher
David Gascoyne
Ivor Gurney
David Harsent
Gwen Harwood
Anthony Hecht
Zbigniew Herbert
Thomas Kinsella
Brad Leithauser
Derek Mahon

Jamie McKendrick
Sean O'Brien
Peter Porter
Craig Raine
Henry Reed
Christopher Reid
Stephen Romer
Carole Satyamurti
Peter Scupham
Jo Shapcott
Penelope Shuttle
Anne Stevenson
George Szirtes
Grete Tartler
Edward Thomas
Charles Tomlinson
Chris Wallace-Crabbe
Hugo Williams